I0845479

# DEDICATION

This book is dedicated to all the amazing animals, big and small, predator and prey.

ACKNOWLEDGEMENTS

I'd like to thank my family, and teacher, who
have supported me in the making of the
very book you are reading right now.

# CONTENTS

# About Them

The cheetah is the skillful speedster of the savanna. The cheetah's scientific name is Acinonyx Jubatus. The Asiatic cheetah's scientific name is Acinonyx Jubatus Venaticus. Cheetahs live mostly in Africa but there is a small population of Asiatic cheetahs living in Iran. Cheetahs grow to be about 55 kilograms to 65 kilograms in weight and are about two to three metres long. However, cheetahs are most well known for their incredible sprinting speeds, up to 110 kilometres per hour and accelerating from 0 to 70 kilometres per hour in less than three seconds. Their long, thin legs and unusually long spine allows it to cover over 6.4 metres in a single stride.

# Their Habitat

Cheetahs live in northern, eastern and southern Africa but they are most prevalent in Kenya and Tanzania in east Africa, and Namibia and Botswana in Southern Africa. However, Asiatic Cheetahs live in small isolated groups in the most remote places of Iran where they remain critically endangered. Sometimes, coalitions live in small 30 square kilometre territories; in other areas, they can have up to 1500 square kilometres of territory.

An ironic fact is that cheetahs actually need lions, who are their biggest predator, to survive. Lions will kill adult and young cheetah whenever they get the chance to do so. Lions are like unintentional bodyguards keeping other unwanted predators like leopards, hyenas, jackals and crocodiles away.

Some of the main essentials for a cheetah's territory are an abundance of prey, preferably small gazelles and impalas, but also the young of larger prey, like warthogs, wildebeest, and kudus. They need water, but not a lot because cheetahs only need to drink every three to four days. They also need good vantage points like hills and tall trees to climb, to look over the savanna for a tasty meal.

Shelter from the sun and heat is also needed with cheetahs spending around 88% of their day resting and getting ready for their next hunt. The heat where most cheetahs live can reach staggering temperatures and it's super dry.

# Fun Fact #1

Cheetahs' numbers have dropped drastically over the past century from 100,000 in the 1900s with them living in India and Kazakhstan, and most of Africa. The current population was just a little over 7,000 in 2010. Cheetahs, both African and Asiatic Cheetahs, no longer live in 91% of their historic range and are scattered around Africa and in very small areas of Iran. Even with them being a protected species, humans keep encroaching on the cheetah's wild habitat and territory making them a vulnerable species in Africa and critically endangered in Asia.

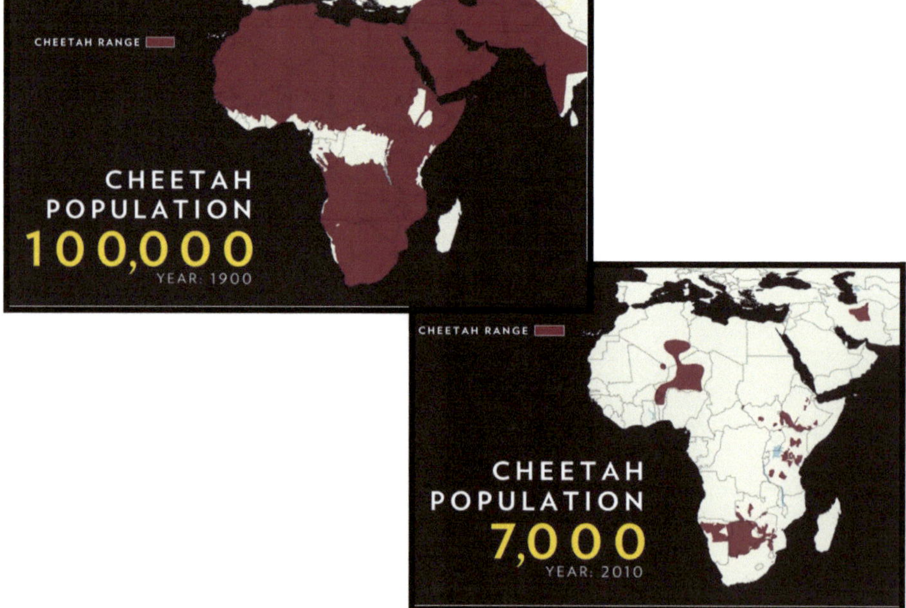

# Prey

Cheetahs are big critics when it comes to food, only eating fresh kills and never carrion. These wild cats can only take down small or medium sized prey like rodents, hares, impalas, gazelles, springbok, and sometimes the calves of larger animals.

Coalitions, made up of males, usually brothers, form lifelong hunting teams of around  two to five individuals. This makes hunts much more successful and rewarding with larger prey, more often. In coalitions, they can now take down adult wildebeests, large antelope, like kudus and oryxes, and even full grown ostriches. Because cheetahs rely on speed for hunting, they require lots of oxygen and have evolved to have small light skulls to make room for large nasal passages. They kill by choking and strangling their prey with their small, but effective, canine teeth.

# Fun Fact #2

Due to how fast they run, about 110 kilometres per hour, cheetahs can only run for about 45 seconds or they may overheat or even die of exhaustion. Once they have caught their prey, they need to rest at least 30 minutes before they can eat. This makes them extremely vulnerable to attacks from a cheetah's predators like lions, leopards, hyenas, large reptiles, jackals, and some birds of prey. On the bright side, cheetahs are one of the most successful big cats when it comes to hunting. They land a meal about once every two tries giving them a 50% success rate.

# **Predators**

Surprisingly, one of the things cheetahs need to survive is also one of their biggest threats, lions. Lions will kill adult and young cheetahs whenever they get the chance to do so, but cheetahs can usually outrun them and escape from their deadly jaws. Lions are unknowingly like bodyguards keeping other unwanted predators like leopards, hyenas, jackals and crocodiles away. Another way cheetahs avoid lions is by hunting at different times. Cheetahs generally hunt during the day while lions prefer to hunt at night. Cheetahs and lions both rest for most of the day therefore creating an even smaller chance of being lion food.

Some mistakes predators make is to mess with a mother cheetah. Her number one job is to protect them no matter what. She must fend and fight off other predators that are usually larger than mom. So finding and changing hiding spots like tall grass or a hidden cave is a top priority.

# The Fur

A cheetah is covered with black spots everywhere except for its stomach, with each cat having its own distinctive pattern and number of spots dappling its body. The tear marks under a cheetah's eyes aren't from crying but for better vision. The black marks may help reduce glare off the cheetah's eyes in order to see better much like the eye black of professional athletes. They also have a few rings instead of spots, on the end of their tails.

Cheetahs are sometimes misidentified as leopards which is an understandable mistake due to their similar shape, size, and they are both spotted but there are some easy ways to identify them. First of all, cheetahs don't spend as much time in the trees as leopards but will sometimes climb one for a better vantage point. Another difference is that cheetahs are slightly smaller and more on average while leopards are bulky and stronger. Finally, cheetahs have small oval and round shaped dots, whereas the leopard has distinctive spots covering its fur called rosettes.

# Fun Fact #3

While most cheetahs have small round spots, there is a small group of cheetahs, called king cheetahs, with a very different looking pattern. Although it was thought to be, it is not a different subspecies but a recessive gene in the cheetah's DNA, most commonly found in southern Africa. In simpler terms, a king cheetah is like having blue or green eyes in an entire family of people with brown eyes.

# Attack and Defence

One the most well known trait of the cheetah is its speed and camouflage. The fur pattern of the cheetah breaks up the outline of it to hide from predators and sneak up on prey. On the other hand, their supernatural speed helps them get away from predators if found or to pursue their speedy prey.

How do cheetahs reach such high speeds so quickly? Well their spine plays a key role, proportionally the longest and most flexible of any large cat species which is extremely important because it enables the cheetah to maximise their stride length. Another thing about them is how steady they keep their head when they're running, its neck is stretched out and its head staying in almost the exact same position. Their large nasal passages, big heart, and huge lungs allow them to bring more oxygen and blood around their body to go as fast as they can.

Another secret to their speed is their tail. The tail of a cheetah acts like a rudder keeping the cheetah balanced while going at such high speeds and not tripping. Cheetahs chase prey that are also really fast and love to twist and turn to get the predator off their tail but the cheetah is the only big cat that is able turn mid-air and once they're close enough, they stick their paw out to trip the fleeing prey. They also have rough paws and semi-retractable claws for the best traction possible.

# Fun Fact #4

A cat has an organ called the Jacobson's organ that acts like a second nose. It's made up of two fluid sacs above the roof of its mouth. It detects scent chemicals or pheromones left behind by other cats. When Jacobson's organ detects the chemicals that are like coded messages, it sends that information up to the brain to learn that there is a cat intruder or a cat looking for a mate.

# Relatives

Cheetahs are currently one of the seven big cats which include lions, tigers, jaguars, leopards, snow leopards, cougars, and cheetahs. They are the only big cats that aren't able to fully retract their claws. They are also the smallest members of the big cats. Cheetahs are one of the only big cats apart from cougars to have a genus name that doesn't start with panthera but Acinonyx. There are a total of 41 wildcat species with 34 of them not being big cats but small and medium sized ones. The cheetah's closest relatives are the cougar and jaguarundi. The three of them together create the puma lineage, which branched off from the other cats around 6.7 mya.

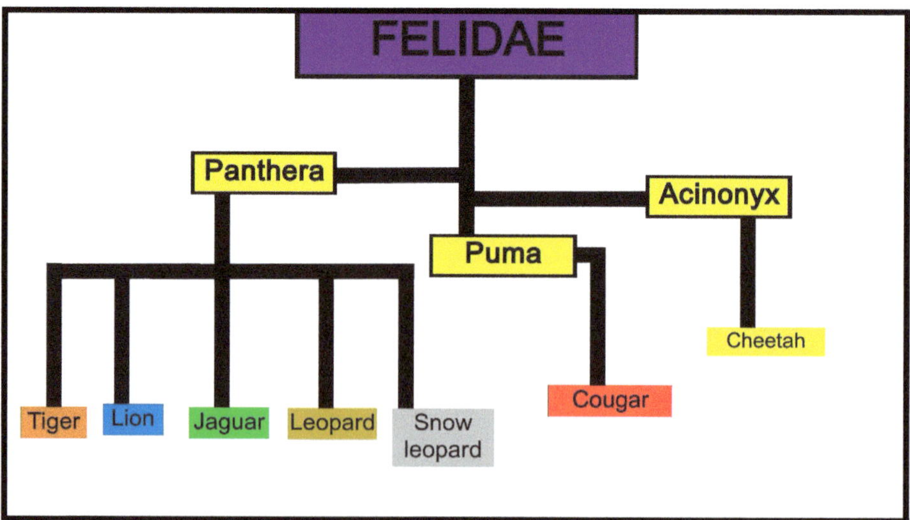

# Fun Fact #5

Everyone knows that your household tabby goes crazy for catnip, but they're not the only ones. In the 1970s, zoologists gave catnip to 33 big cats at a zoo in Tennessee, USA. The Jaguars and Lions had the biggest reactions playing in it for an hour and were far more responsive than a housecat that just spent around 15 minutes in the mint like plant matter. Tigers, cougars and bobcats were less interested and the cheetahs just ignored it completely.

# Mating

Breeding occurs throughout the year. Females are polyestrous, with a typical estrous cycle lasting 12 days in which the female will be "in heat" for 1 to 3 days. Female cheetahs may mate with more than one male. Mating may  occur immediately and copulations last less than a minute. They may stay together for a few days and mate several more times during this period, an average of 3 to 5 times per day.

# The Cubs

Cheetahs give birth to 2 to 8 cubs at a time 3 to 5 is the most common amount. All big cat moms bond with their cubs for the first few days by licking them from head to tail, and it's also a way to clean them and hide the scent of newborns. Newborn cheetah cubs only weigh around 150 to 400 grams, that's less than five percent of their mother's weight, easily fitting into a human hand.

Cheetah cubs are blind for the first seven to ten days and are completely helpless relying on their mother to give them protection, warmth, and food. Because the cubs are still helpless and slow if danger comes, mom will carry the cubs by the scruff of their neck that triggers a natural reflex that causes them to go limp and become easier and more to carry.

Due to the fact that cheetahs have to travel far to find food and maybe successfully hunt it, cheetahs are the youngest big cats to venture from the den. Because they leave so early, they are unable to outrun or fight a predator like a lion. However, cheetahs have evolved an adaptation that only happens when they are cubs, and it's called mimicry. Honey badgers are debatably the fiercest animals on the African savanna, even lions and top predators try to steer clear of them. They have a distinctive thick white stripe running along their back like the ones of skunks marking a clear warning sign to not get close. When cheetahs are cubs, they also have a white stripe called a mantle that looks like a honey badger's. Therefore, when a predator is near, all a cub has to do is hide its face and show its back to mimic a honey badger's. This stripe starts to fade at four months of age and disappears when it's around 12 months old.

# Are They Endangered?

Cheetahs have faced many challenges over the past century and still to this day. Cheetahs are going extinct due to poaching, climate change, human encroachment, the loss of prey from poaching of other animals, retaliation for livestock attack, trophy hunting, captured and sold as pets, and vehicular accidents. These charming cats are sadly vulnerable in most parts of Africa but are critically endangered in North Africa and Asia.

The good news is that their numbers have grown to around 7100 individuals compared to the 7000 cheetahs ten years ago in 2010. Even though their numbers have grown with the help of many amazing organizations like National Geographic and the WWF. There is still a long way to go seeing that the numbers were over 100,000 a century ago, this is still a good start. It's sad that this is a reality but there are some things you can do to help.

You could help by:

- Starting a penny drive or sell cookies to raise money and donate it to some awesome conservations
- Tell your family and friends to spread awareness about cheetahs and how to protect them
- "Adopt" a cheetah on marvellous organisations like National Geographic, WWF, CCF, and many others.
- Don't buy souvenirs made of cheetahs or any animals

# Famous Cheetahs

Cheetahs are quite famous with a bunch you may already know about. From the Children's cartoon series, Wild Kratts, there is Blur and Spotswat. Officer Benjamin Clawhauser who is the chubby cheetah from Disney's Zootopia. Wearing his iconic sunglasses and white shoes, Chester cheetah is the classic Cheetos mascot.

The Tano Bora, also known as the Fast Five was a coalition of five cheetahs with two sadly passing away in 2021 and 2022. They were the largest known cheetah coalition to exist which caught the attention of many people including wildlife photographers and filmmakers. Tano Bora means Magnificent Five in the Swahili language. They were captivating with their stealth, strategy, and striking beauty in Masai Mara, their home. However, the most remarkable thing was that only two of them were brothers.

# Random Cheetah Facts

- Asiatic cheetahs have been kept in captivity for more than 4000 years. They were the easiest big cats to tame, and rulers, including Genghis Khan, used them as hunting partners.

- A cheetah is covered in about two to three thousand inky black spots.

- According to African legend, the black marks on a cheetah's face are tear stains because it can't figure out if it's a cat or dog.

- Cheetahs are unable to roar but they are the only big cats to chirp.

- A cheetah's heart rate and blood pressure becomes higher after a kill most likely due to stress of another animal wanting to steal the fresh food.

- Around 75% of cheetah cubs don't make it to their first year which is why cheetahs have evolved into having larger litters.

- Their scientific name for the cheetah is Acinonyx Jubatus with Acinonyx literally meaning "no move claw" in greek.

- A cheetah typically gets a football field's width away from its prey before engaging with the chase.

- An effective way of protecting livestock and cheetahs was to place Kangal and Anatolian shepherds as herding and guard dogs to scare away the cheetahs and keep them away.

# Explain the Words

**Abundance:** An extremely plentiful or over sufficient quantity or supply.

**Accelerate:** To cause faster or greater activity, advancement, development, etc.

**Adaptation:** A change or process to change by which an organism becomes better suited for its environment.

**Coalition:** The group name for cheetahs.

**Distinctive:** Different, unique.

**DNA:** Deoxyribonucleic acid is the molecule that carries genetic information for the development and functioning of an organism.

**Encroachment:** Intrusion of someone or something's territory or area.

**Endangered:** At risk of becoming extinct.

**Mimicry:** close external resemblance of an organism to a different organism.

**Nasal:** Of or relating to the nose.

**Polyestrous:** Having several breeding cycles annually or during breeding seasons.

**Prevalent:** Widespread; of wide extent or occurrence.

**Recessive:** Both genes in a pair or both parents must carry the abnormal gene to cause a disease or mutation.

**Retaliation:** Revenge.

**Vantage:** A position, condition or place affording some advantage or commanding view.

**Vehicular:** Of, relating to or for vehicles.

**Vulnerable:** A species becoming at risk of extinction.

# About the Author

"What Cat is That? Cheetahs" is Evan Ren's fifth book. His first, "Escape from Mirantibus" is the fictional story of brother and sister Greg and Willa, who did odd jobs, ran errands, scrimped and saved for their dream cruise.

The cruise is going well… until a superpod of dolphins comes along.

In the excitement, the unthinkable happens and someone goes overboard, leading to adventures beyond their imagination.

After "Escape from Mirantibus" Evan started the "What Cat is That?" series of books with the first volume, "Leopards". This was followed up by his books on Lions, and Tigers, and the book you are reading which is, of course, Cheetahs!

Evan Ren is an author based in West Vancouver, Canada. He has been writing since he was 10 years old. At the time of this publication he is the advanced age of 12 with five books to his name already.

Evan has a five-year old brother, Max, and a three-year old sister, Leah, He also has a dog who likes to bark.  Aside from having an affinity for writing at a young age, he also likes basketball and soccer. When asked what his favourite food is he said he can't say because his mom makes so many good dishes he can't choose just one. When Evan finishes school he would like to work in a wildlife animal shelter.

www.ingramcontent.com/pod-product-compliance
Lightning Source LLC
Chambersburg PA
CBHW040318240726
48664CB00006B/1533